Fun at the Park
by Ruth Owen

Editorial consultant: Mitch Cronick

New Forest Press

CONTENTS

Words in **bold** are explained in the glossary.

Fun at the Park

It is fun to go to the park.

There is always lots to do.

Spring in the Park

It is **spring**.

There are many things to see and do.

green leaves

tulips

flower buds

7

Spring Ducklings

The ducks lay eggs in the spring.

The ducklings **hatch** from the eggs.

duck

ducklings

9

Summer in the Park

You can have a picnic in the **summer**.

At the Playground

You can go to the playground.

slide

12

swing

13

Fall Fun

It is **fall**.

The leaves fall off the trees.

leaves

Fall Seeds

The trees have **seeds**.

You can collect them.

acorn

17

Winter in the Park

You can sled in the **winter**.

18

Sledding is fun!

19

Snow!

It snows in winter.

You can make a snowman.

snowman

21

Glossary

fall

We divide a year into spring, summer, fall, and winter. Fall is when trees drop their leaves, and the weather gets cool.

hatch
To break out of an egg

seeds
Small parts of plants that will grow into new plants

spring

We divide a year into spring, summer, fall, and winter. Spring is when new plants grow. Many animals have babies in spring.

summer

We divide a year into spring, summer, fall, and winter. Summer is when the weather gets warm.

winter

We divide a year into spring, summer, fall, and winter. Winter is when many plants die, and the weather gets cold.

Index

Publisher: Tim Cook
Editor: Valerie J. Weber
Designer: Matt Harding

ISBN: 978 1 84898 500 1
Library of Congress Control Number: 2011924951

U.S. publication © 2011 New Forest Press
Published in arrangement with Black Rabbit Books

PO Box 784, Mankato, MN 56002

www.newforestpress.com
Printed in the USA
15 14 13 12 11 1 2 3 4 5

Picture credits (t=top, b=bottom, c=center, l=left, r=right):
iStock: 1, 8t, 16, 20–21, 22t. Shutterstock: front cover, 2, 4–5 (all), 6–7, 7t, 8–9, 10–11, 12, 13,
14–15 (all), 17, 18-19, 20, 22b, 23t, back cover (all)

Every effort has been made to trace the copyright holders, and we apologize in advance for any unintentional omissions.
We would be pleased to insert the appropriate acknowledgements in any subsequent edition of this publication.

24